SUPER SIMPLE

INDIAN ART

FUN AND EASY ART FROM AROUND THE WORLD

ALEX KUSKOWSKI

Super Sandcastle

An Imprint of Abdo Publishing
www.abdopublishing.com

Consulting Editor, Diane Craig,
M.A./Reading Specialist

VISIT US AT WWW.ABDOPUBLISHING.COM

Published by Abdo Publishing, a division of ABDO, PO Box 398166, Minneapolis, Minnesota 55439. Copyright © 2015 by Abdo Consulting Group, Inc. International copyrights reserved in all countries. No part of this book may be reproduced in any form without written permission from the publisher. Super SandCastle™ is a trademark and logo of Abdo Publishing.

Printed in the United States of America, North Mankato, Minnesota
062014
092014

THIS BOOK CONTAINS RECYCLED MATERIALS

Editor: Liz Salzmann
Content Developer: Nancy Tuminelly
Cover and Interior Design and Production: Mighty Media, Inc.
Photo Credits: Aaron DeYoe, Shutterstock

The following manufacturers/names appearing in this book are trademarks: Crayola®, Crystal Sugar®, Elmer's®, 3M™ Scotch®, FabricMate, Y&C, Sanalac®, Mod Podge®, Ziploc®, Velcro®, Roundy's®

Library of Congress Cataloging-in-Publication Data
Kuskowski, Alex., author.
  Super simple Indian art : fun and easy art from around the world / Alex Kuskowski ; consulting editor, Diane Craig, M.A., reading specialist.
    pages cm. -- (Super simple cultural art)
  Audience: Ages 5-10.
  ISBN 978-1-62403-280-6
1. Handicraft--Juvenile literature. 2. Art, Indic--Juvenile literature. 3. India--Civilization-
-Miscellanea--Juvenile literature. I. Craig, Diane, editor. II. Title. III. Series: Super simple cultural art.
  TT103.K87 2015
  745.50954--dc23
                    2013043676

TO ADULT HELPERS

Children can have a lot of fun learning about different cultures through arts and crafts. Be sure to supervise them as they work on the projects in this book. Let the kids do as much as possible on their own. But be ready to step in and help if necessary. Also, kids may be using glue, paint, markers, and clay. Make sure they protect their clothes and work surfaces.

KEY SYMBOLS

In this book you may see some **symbols**. Here are what they mean.

SHARP!
You will be working with a sharp object. Get help.

HOT!
You will be working with something hot. Get help.

TABLE OF CONTENTS

GHUNGROOS

Ghungroos are Indian ankle bells. Dancers wear them to make music while they move.

COOL CULTURE

Get ready to go on a **cultural** art adventure! All around the world, people make art. They use art to show different **traditions** and ideas. Learning about different cultures with art can be a lot of fun.

India is a country in **Asia**. It has many different traditions and cultures. The Indian government **recognizes** more than 20 languages. More than one **billion** people live in India!

Learn more about India! Try some of the art projects in this book. Get creative with culture using art.

BEFORE YOU START

Remember to treat other people and **cultures** with respect. Respect their art, **jewelry**, and clothes too. These things can have special meaning to people.

There are a few rules for doing art projects:

▶ **PERMISSION**
Make sure to get **permission** to do a project. You might want to use things you find around the house. Ask first!

▶ **SAFETY**
Get help from an adult when using something hot or sharp. Never use a stove or oven by yourself.

ART IN INDIAN CULTURE

People in India create many beautiful things. Some are for everyday use. Others are for special occasions. The **designs** in Indian art often have special meanings.

A mandala is a special **design** shaped like a circle. Mandalas stand for the universe.

Diwali is a holiday that usually happens in the fall. People light lamps and share sweets to celebrate.

Batik is a way of decorating cloth. People use dye and wax to make patterns on cloth.

The sacred lotus is the national flower of India. It stands for great beauty.

Henna is a dye. People use it to decorate their skin. It can take up to a month for it to wear off.

Nan Khatai are a kind of Indian cookie. These sweet treats are from western India.

In India, people sometimes hang torans over their doors. People put them up to mark important events.

Bangles are part of **traditional** Indian **jewelry**. **Bangles** are often made out of colored glass.

WHAT YOU NEED

acrylic paint, foam
brush & paintbrush

air-dry clay

almonds &
cardamom powder

baking sheet

ball-point pen &
pencil

beads & fake
flowers

brown paper bag

bucket & laundry
soap

butter & sugar

canvas paper

craft glue &
glue gel

craft sticks &
drinking glass

double-sided tape

felt & craft foam

jewels

key chain ring

LED candle

marker & fabric markers

milk powder

mixing bowl & mixing spoon

measuring cups & spoons

Mod Podge

newspaper

paper cup

plastic zipper bag

rolling pin & cookie cutters

ruler

saucepan

scissors

self-adhesive hook-and-loop dots

small jingle bells

string & large needle

sweetened condensed milk & can opener

tissue paper

waxed paper

white t-shirt

wide ribbon

MAGNIFICENT MANDALA

Fold paint into a picture!

pencil

canvas paper

ruler

scissors

newspaper

white, yellow, red & blue
acrylic paint

DIRECTIONS

1. Draw a circle 10 inches (25.5 cm) across on the canvas paper. Cut out the circle. Fold the circle in half. Fold the half circle in half. Fold the quarter circle in half. Cut across the curved edge of the paper to make a triangle. Unfold the paper.

2. Fold the paper in half along each of the folds, one at a time. Press along the folded edges to **crease** them. Unfold the paper.

3. Cover your work area with newspaper. Put small dots of paint all over the paper.

4. Fold the paper in half along each of the folds, one at a time. Unfold the paper. Let the paint dry for 6 hours.

ANKLE BELLS

Make music while you dance!

WHAT YOU NEED

felt

ruler

scissors

string

large needle

small jingle bells

self-adhesive hook-and-loop dot

DIRECTIONS

1. Cut a strip of felt 12 inches (30.5 cm) by 2 inches (5 cm).

2. Thread a piece of string through the needle. Push the needle through the felt.

3. Slide a bell over the needle. Push the needle back through the felt. Remove the needle. Tie the string in a knot. Cut off any extra string.

4. Sew on more bells. Sew them in a row with ½ inch (1.3 cm) between them. Leave about 1 inch (2.5 cm) between the last bell and the end of the felt.

5. Separate the hook-and-loop dot. Stick one side of the dot to the space at the end of the bells. Turn the felt over. Stick the other side of the dot near the other end of the felt.

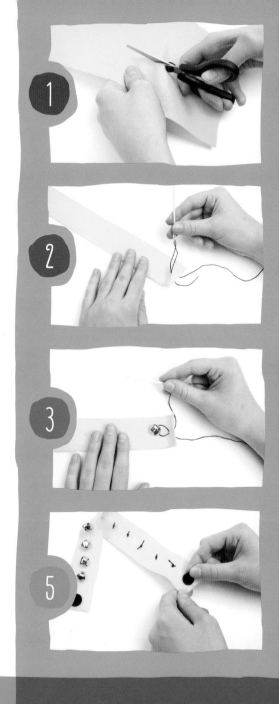

FLOWER HANGING

Decorate your doorway!

WHAT YOU NEED

string

ruler

scissors

large needle

wide red ribbon,
4 feet (1.2 m) long

fake flowers

red, yellow, and orange
beads

DirecTIONS

1. Cut five pieces of string 10 inches (25.5 cm) long. Cut four pieces of string 5 inches (12.7 cm) long. Tie a knot at one end of each string.

2. Thread a long string onto the needle. Push the needle through the ribbon. Put 7 inches (18 cm) of beads and flowers on the string.

3. Push thread back through the ribbon about 4 inches (10 cm) away. Tie the string in a knot.

4. Thread a short string onto the needle. Push the needle through the ribbon near the first string. Put 3 inches (7.6 cm) of beads and a flower on the string. Tie a knot in the end of the string.

5. Repeat steps 2 through 4 with the remaining strings. Cut off any extra string.

DIWALI BOWL

Fill this cute bowl with wrapped candy!

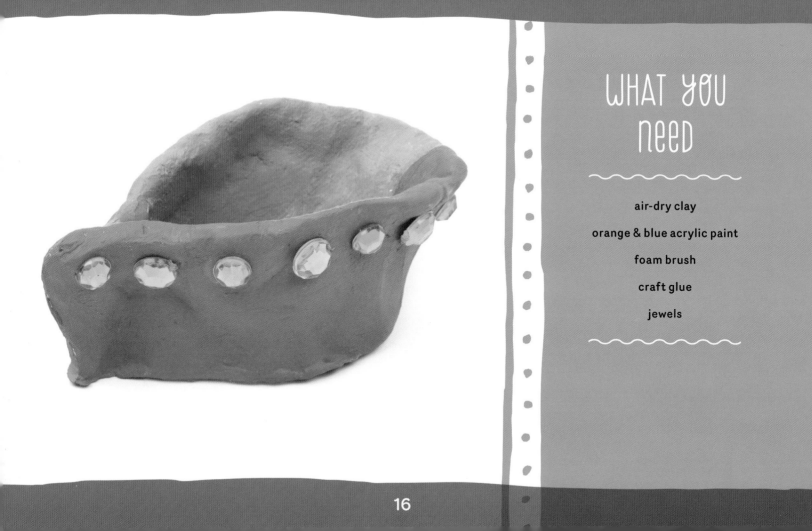

WHAT YOU NEED

air-dry clay

orange & blue acrylic paint

foam brush

craft glue

jewels

DIRECTIONS

1. Roll a ball of clay about the size of your fist. Make a hole in the ball with your thumb. Shape the clay into a bowl. Pinch one end of the bowl with your fingers to make a point. Let the clay dry according to the directions on the package.

2. Paint half of the bowl orange. Let the paint dry. Paint the other half of the bowl blue. Let the paint dry.

3. Glue on **jewels** for decoration.

QUICK TIP: Don't put unwrapped food or candy in your Diwali bowl.

LOVELY LOTUS FLOWER

Let a flower light up your room!

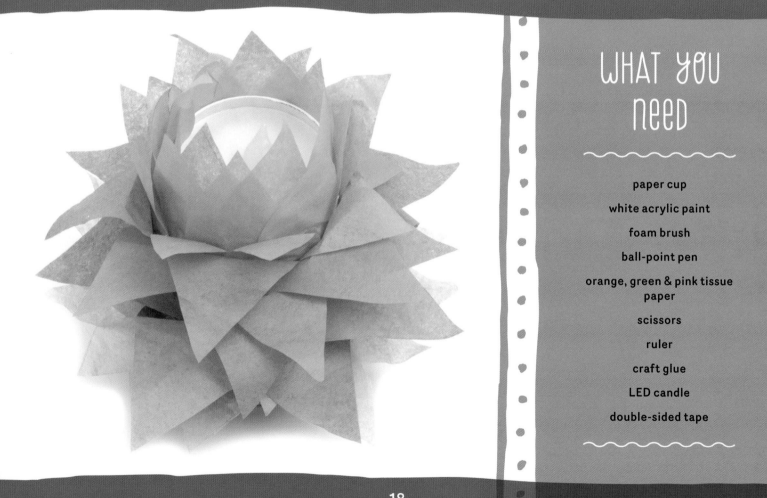

WHAT YOU NEED

paper cup

white acrylic paint

foam brush

ball-point pen

orange, green & pink tissue paper

scissors

ruler

craft glue

LED candle

double-sided tape

DIRECTIONS

1. Paint the outside of the paper cup white. Let the paint dry.

2. Poke a hole in the bottom of the cup. Make sure the bulb of the LED candle can fit through the hole.

3. Cut orange and green tissue paper into teardrop shapes. Make the teardrops 2 inches (5 cm) long. Cut pink tissue paper into teardrop shapes. Make the pink teardrops 3 inches (7.6 cm) long.

PROJECT CONTINUES ON THE NEXT PAGE

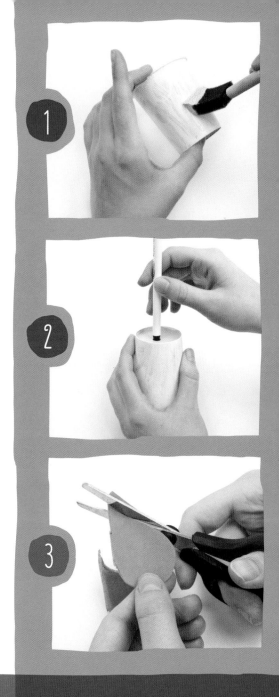

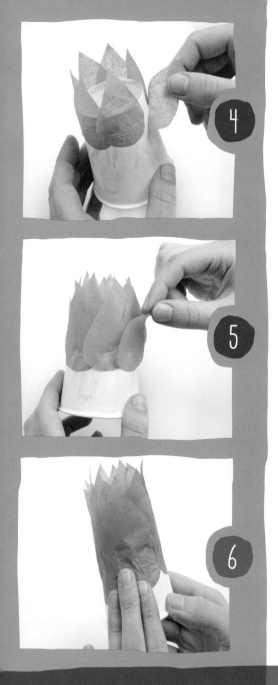

DIRECTIONS (CONTINUED)

(4) Turn the cup upside down. Brush glue on the rounded end of an orange teardrop. stick it onto the cup pointing up. Press and smooth the paper.

(5) Glue more orange teardrops around the cup. **Overlap** the teardrops. Make another row of teardrops a little lower. Keep adding rows until half the cup is covered.

(6) Glue on rows of pink teardrops. Glue them on the same way as the orange teardrops. Keep adding rows until the cup is almost covered.

DIRECTIONS (continued)

7. Glue a row of green teardrops around the bottom of the cup. Let the glue dry.

8. Fold out the tops of the teardrops to make the flower open. Leave the top rows of orange teardrops pointing up.

9. Put two strips of double-sided tape on the top of the LED candle.

10. Put the LED light inside the cup. Push the bulb through the hole in the cup. Press the candle against the inside of the cup until the tape sticks. Turn the cup back over.

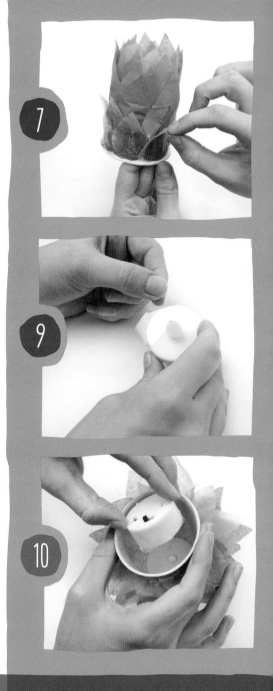

BEAUTIFUL BANGLES

Make a rocking bracelet!

WHAT YOU NEED

saucepan

measuring cup

craft sticks

drinking glass

acrylic paint

paintbrush

jewels

Mod Podge

foam brush

DIRECTIONS

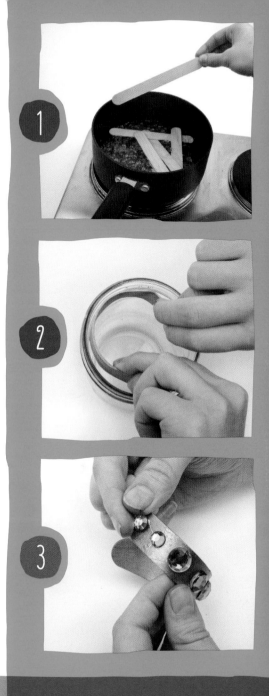

1. Put 3 cups of water in a saucepan. Have an adult help you bring the water to a boil. Add craft sticks. Boil for 30 minutes. Take the pan off the heat. Let it sit for 30 minutes.

2. Remove the craft sticks from the pan. Slowly bend each stick into a circle. Fit them around the inside of the drinking glass. Let them dry for 6 hours. Take them out of the glass.

3. Decorate the **bangles**. Paint fun **designs**. Let the paint dry. Glue on **jewels**.

4. Paint the bangles with a coat of Mod Podge. Let the glue dry.

PEACOCK SHIRT PRINT

Make a shirt that stands out!

WHAT YOU NEED

newspaper

brown paper bag

white T-shirt

pencil

Elmer's blue glue gel

fabric markers

bucket

laundry soap

DIRECTIONS

1   Cover your work area with newspaper.

2   Put the brown paper bag inside the shirt. Lay the shirt flat on the newspaper.

3   Draw a peacock in pencil on the shirt. Trace the pencil lines with glue. Let it dry for 6 hours.

4   Paint the peacock with fabric markers. Let the paint dry for 6 hours.

5   Wash the shirt with soap and water. Let dry.

HENNA KEY CHAIN

Let your key chain give you a hand!

WHAT YOU NEED

thin craft foam

ball-point pen

ruler

scissors

brown marker

large needle

red, blue & yellow string

key chain ring

DIRECTIONS

1. Draw a hand on the foam. Make it 3 inches (7.6 cm) high. Cut out the hand. Draw a henna **design** with the brown marker.

2. Poke a hole near the bottom edge of the palm.

3. Cut one piece each of blue, yellow, and red string. Make them 10 inches (25.5 cm) long. Tie the strings together with a knot near one end.

4. Braid the strings together. Tie a knot at the end. Stick the braid through the hole in the hand. Add the key chain ring. Tie the ends of the braid together.

ALMOND COOKIE

Get a bite of this tasty Indian cookie!

WHAT YOU NEED

measuring cups & spoons

½ cup almonds

plastic zipper bag

rolling pin

½ cup butter

mixing bowl

2 cups milk powder

1 can sweetened condensed milk

can opener

¼ cup sugar

mixing spoon

½ teaspoon cardamom powder

waxed paper

cookie cutters

baking sheet

DIRECTIONS

1. Put the almonds in a plastic zipper bag. Roll over them with a rolling pin. Crush them into large pieces.

2. Put the butter in a bowl. Microwave it for 20 seconds.

3. Add the milk powder, condensed milk, and sugar to the bowl. Stir well.

4. Microwave the mixture for 1 minute. Take it out and stir it. Microwave and stir the mixture three more times.

PROJECT CONTINUES ON THE NEXT PAGE

DIRECTIONS (CONTINUED)

(5) Add the cardamom and almonds.

(6) Stir well. Let the mixture cool.

(7) Lay out a piece of waxed paper. Put the cookie **dough** on the waxed paper.

DIRECTIONS (CONTINUED)

(8) Roll the **dough** with a rolling pin until it is ½ inch (1.3 cm) thick.

(9) Use cookie cutters to cut out shapes.

10 Repeat steps 8 and 9 until the dough is all used up.

(11) Place the cookies on a baking sheet. Chill them in the refrigerator for 30 minutes.

GLOSSARY

Asia – the largest of the continents. Russia, India, and China are in Asia.

bangle – a stiff band worn around the wrist or ankle.

billion – a very large number. One billion is also written 1,000,000,000.

crease – to make a sharp line in something by folding it.

culture – the ideas, art, and other products of a particular group of people.

design – a decorative pattern or arrangement.

dough – a thick mixture of flour, water, and other ingredients used in baking.

jewel – a precious stone such as an emerald or a diamond.

jewelry – pretty things, such as rings and necklaces, that you wear for decoration.

overlap – to make something lie partly on top of something else.

permission – when a person in charge says it's okay to do something.

recognize – to officially accept.

symbol – an object or picture that stands for or represents something.

tradition – a belief or practice passed through a family or group of people.